IMAGES
of America

THE WAUPACA
CHAIN O' LAKES

By 1942, the Waupaca Chain o' Lakes had become so popular among tourists that the Curt Teich Company of Chicago created one of its famous "Greetings from" postcards to advertise them. The postcard includes scenes that could be of any rural lake but still shows the lakes as "the ideal spot for the camera enthusiast, the swimmer, the boater, and the fisherman," as a *Chicago Tribune* journalist described them in 1949. (Author's collection.)

ON THE COVER: This photograph from 1905 depicts Roy Holly and friends aboard his canoe, the *Rob Roy*, on Beasley Lake. Early vacationers loved canoeing on the Chain o' Lakes because of the scenic shores and calm waters and spent days exploring the many lakes and channels, sometimes traversing all of them in single outings. (Waupaca Historical Society.)

IMAGES
of America

THE WAUPACA CHAIN O' LAKES

Zachary Bishop
Foreword by Elmer Keil

ARCADIA
PUBLISHING

Copyright © 2020 by Zachary Bishop
ISBN 978-1-4671-0431-9

Published by Arcadia Publishing
Charleston, South Carolina

Library of Congress Control Number: 2019948050

For all general information, please contact Arcadia Publishing:
Telephone 843-853-2070
Fax 843-853-0044
E-mail sales@arcadiapublishing.com
For customer service and orders:
Toll-Free 1-888-313-2665

Visit us on the Internet at www.arcadiapublishing.com

In loving memory of my grandparents, Gladys and Russell Kraemer, who filled our family's vacations on the Chain o' Lakes with so much fun, laughter, and love. Their enthusiasm for life lives on in our hearts and minds.

CONTENTS

FOREWORD

I moved to Waupaca in June 1963, when my parents, Otto and Genevieve Keil, bought the Pines Inn Resort on McCrossen Lake, one of the 22 Chain o' Lakes. Before that, we lived in Franklin Park, Illinois, and had been coming to the Waupaca area for many years to attend Camp Shin-Go-Beek, the Boy Scouts' summer camp near Wild Rose. I first went as a scout and later as a counselor.

In March 1964, I started my career as a plumber with Cook Plumbing and Heating in Waupaca. When I finished my apprenticeship, I moved on to being a journeyman plumber and master plumber for Local Union 458 in Appleton, later Local Union 400. I married Sandy Olson of Waupaca on October 11, 1969, and celebrated 50 years of marriage with her in 2019 along with four other couples from the area. We have two sons, Jerad and Matt, and welcomed their wives, six grandchildren, and two step-grandchildren into our family.

For many years, Sandy and I owned and rented out the first two units of the Pines Inn Resort and lived on a house on McCrossen Lake. That is how I met Zach Bishop when he was a baby. His grandparents, aunt, uncles, and mom started spending their two-week vacations at the units in 1979, and his parents continued the tradition. As he grew up, he was always precise with all of the projects he worked on. He wrote his college thesis on the Chain o' Lakes and did all of the research while he was here on vacation with his family.

During the winter and spring of 2019, he traveled from his home in Illinois to Waupaca on weekends to do research and scan historical photographs. He talked with several people who know the Chain o' Lakes area's history well and worked with the Waupaca Historical Society. Zach has made sure that all of his research is accurate in terms of dates, names, and facts. I hope you enjoy reading his work.

—Elmer Keil

ACKNOWLEDGMENTS

I am indebted to so many wonderful people and organizations for helping me turn my dream of publishing a book on the Chain o' Lakes into a reality. The Waupaca Historical Society board of directors graciously allowed me to fill most of these pages with historical photographs from their collection. Longtime volunteer JJ Johnson and executive director Tracy Behrendt were a tremendous help with finding research resources for me. In addition, the resources of the Waupaca Area Genealogical Society and Waupaca Area Public Library greatly aided me in my research.

Numerous individuals kindly shared their knowledge, memories, and images of the Chain o' Lakes for the book, including Ron Arthur, Mike Kirk, Joe and Ginny Leean, Al and Nancy Oftedahl, Bob and Mary Ann Wells, Helen Potts Robinson, Kent Pegorsch, Georgia Calvo, Mark Ilten, Jeff Jenswold, Joel Jenswold, Jan Jenswold, Skip Bonnell, Jack Bonnell, Kristi Diaz, June Melby, and so many others. The wonderful staff at the Jesuit Archives & Research Center, Boys' and Girls' Brigade, Wisconsin Historical Society, and History Nebraska also provided me with wonderful photographs and research assistance.

My dear friends Sandy and Elmer Keil connected me with local experts and collectors and hosted me during research trips. Elmer also wrote a wonderful foreword for the book. My phenomenal mom, Jill, accompanied me on research trips and supported me every step of the way. The rest of my exceptional family and friends cheered me on and kept me sane, especially Dad, Shannon, Uncle Glenn, Aunt Cyndi, Aunt Joy, Aunt Brenda, Ngaire, Ash, and Lee.

I am beyond grateful to Arcadia Publishing for giving me the opportunity to write this book. Their phenomenal staff, especially Caitrin Cunningham and Jeff Ruetsche, did a wonderful job guiding me through the publishing process and helping me to create a great finished product.

For the sake of clarity, I have identified all lakes and landmarks in the Chain o' Lakes area by their present-day names. I also used initials to credit photographs shared with me courtesy of the Waupaca Historical Society (WHS) and the Boys' and Girls' Brigade of Neenah (BGB).

INTRODUCTION

As a child, every year I counted down the days until my family's annual two-week vacation to the Waupaca Chain o' Lakes. I loved swimming through McCrossen Lake's crystal-clear water, spending hours playing games with my cousins on the swim raft, taking paddleboat rides to the "Slow No Wake" buoy, and staying in the peaceful units of the Pines Inn Resort. As I grew up, I survived many canoe trips down the Crystal River's wild rapids, ate hundreds of ice-cream cones at Scoopers, and took as many boat rides as possible, making precious memories with my family and friends in the process.

Thousands of families like mine have vacationed on the 22 bodies of water that make up the Chain o' Lakes since the 1880s, with many making it an annual—and, over time, multigenerational—tradition. Although the buildings, technology, supplies, and clothing used by tourists and locals have changed dramatically, the lakes have never stopped enchanting the hearts of all who spend time at them.

The history of people interacting with the Chain o' Lakes is fascinating. Native Americans camped, hunted, and practiced their religions on the shores of the lakes, followed by European American settlers who built lives farming the area's fertile soil. Later, locals—and businesspeople from elsewhere—started hotels, restaurants, boat liveries, and fun attractions on "the Chain" that ranged from practical and ordinary to extravagant and bizarre. Vacationers began to visit and continued visiting the lakes to be close to nature, engage in hobbies, have fun with family and friends, escape the stress of daily life, and improve their minds, bodies, and spirits.

The City of Waupaca and its residents played a huge role in the development and continued prosperity of the Chain o' Lakes despite the city being located about three miles to the northeast. After persuading the Wisconsin Central Railroad to lay its tracks through Waupaca in 1871, the city's residents marketed the lakes as a vacation destination for Midwestern tourists and shepherded them from the train depot to the lakes via carriages and, later, an electric trolley line. After the arrival of automobiles in the 1910s, Waupaca continued providing services and attractions for travelers staying at the lakes.

This book covers the history of the Chain o' Lakes from prehistory to the present day, mainly focusing on the century between 1880 and 1980. To the best of my ability, I have covered almost every important person, event, business, and attraction in the history of the lakes and shared stories that I hope are representative of tourists' experiences in every era.

My favorite slogan used by advertisers of the Chain o' Lakes is: "In All The World, No Lakes Like These!" With beautiful scenery, great potential for recreation, delightful tourist attractions and businesses, and interesting locals and visitors, these lakes have been and remain extraordinary.

One

SPRAWLING WATERS

The unique natural characteristics of the Chain o' Lakes have long attracted people to their shores. The lakes formed over 10,000 years ago when large blocks of ice cracked off the retreating Laurentide Ice Sheet and sunk into the flat plains of what became Waupaca County. Melting water, filled with soil and rocks, carved the land around these ice blocks, creating the channels between the lakes and the steep slopes along their shores.

Native Americans called Mound Builders inhabited the Chain o' Lakes area from around 500 BCE to 1100 CE, constructing approximately 75 mounds—for burial and spiritual purposes—around the shores of the lakes. When Europeans started exploring the Wisconsin area, the Menominee Indians were dominant around the lakes and remained so until the mid-19th century, when, through a series of treaties, the Menominee ceded their territory between the Wisconsin, Fox, and Wolf Rivers to the United States. Some remained in the area, but most were forced to move to the Menominee reservation near Shawano in the 1850s.

The Menominee called the Chain o' Lakes *Sīsepikamiw* (pronounced "see-seh-pee-kom-ee"), which translates into "sprawling water, like an animal basking in the sun." Menominee bands from northeastern Wisconsin camped, hunted, and fished around the shores of the lakes, and one band started a settlement near Otter Lake and raised corn.

People from the eastern United States started settling around the Chain o' Lakes in 1849 but did not immediately see them as a valuable natural resource. Five settlers from Vermont claimed land on the present site of Waupaca in June of that year, hoping to harness the Waupaca River to power a mill. Their settlement became the Town of Waupaca when the county was formed in February 1851. Other settlers claimed land around the Chain o' Lakes, organizing the town of Dayton around the southern lakes in December 1852 and Farmington around the northern lakes in April 1853.

Over the course of the Waupaca area's development by these new arrivals during the late 19th century, the physical evidence of Mound Builders' and Menominee lives on the Chain slowly vanished. No photographs or historical drawings showing Native Americans at the lakes have been found.

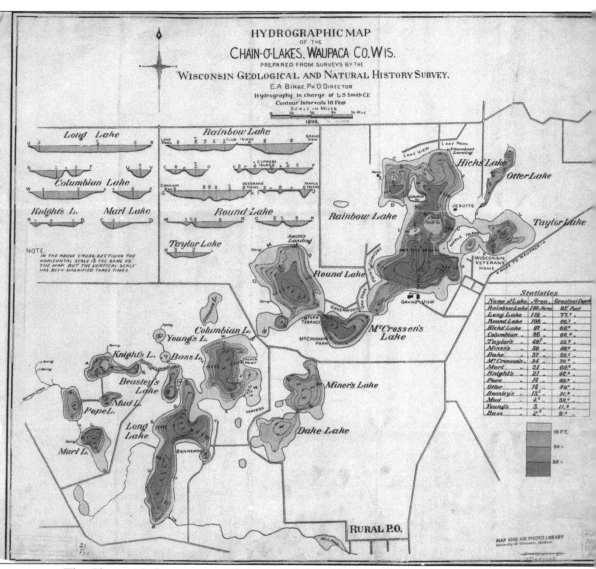

The Chain o' Lakes are naturally beautiful glacial lakes well-suited for swimming and boating. They are small in size but reach depths between 60 and 95 feet at certain points, often sloping quickly downward from the shore, as shown on this 1898 map. Natural springs and Emmons Creek supply the lakes with crystal-clear water, and earthly deposits of marl and organic materials give the lakes' water its blue and green hues. The shores of the lakes are also surrounded by steep bluffs covered in trees that help prevent winds from sweeping across the water. All of the lakes are naturally connected via channels and creeks except for Dake and Miner Lakes, which European American settlers connected to Columbia Lake with a canal. Settlers named most of the lakes after the people who owned land on their shores but named a few lakes based on their unique natural features. (Wisconsin Geological and Natural History Survey.)

HEAD OF EFFIGY INDIAN-MOUND
170 FT. LONG AT CHAIN O'LAKES WAUPACA, WIS.

The Mound Builders who lived on the Chain o' Lakes made several effigy mounds in the shapes of animals and most likely used them for ceremonial purposes. In 1913, the Monday Night Club of Waupaca placed this bronze tablet to mark a 250-foot-long catfish effigy mound near Taylor Lake. This mound remains intact, but most of them were destroyed during the construction of roads and buildings around the start of the 20th century. (WHS.)

Two of the trails that the Menominee Indians and other tribes used to traverse Wisconsin crossed over the channel connecting Limekiln and Columbia Lakes at the point called Indian Crossing. One trail connected the upper Wisconsin River and Lake Poygan, and the other connected Shawano Lake and what became the city of Portage on the Wisconsin River. The Menominee originally waded across the channel but later built a simple log bridge over it. (WHS.)

Niaqtawapomi was the second, or war, chief of the Menominee Tribe under Chief Oshkosh in the 19th century. He was also the acting leader of the Shakitok band, members of which lived slightly northeast of Otter Lake until around 1850. Anthropologist Walter James Hoffman described Niaqtawapomi as "a man of steady habits and influence, and one in whom the tribe has every confidence." This image is originally from Hoffman's book *The Menomini Indians.* (Waupaca Area Public Library.)

This photograph from around 1914 shows Louise Ashmun on Long Lake in a birchbark canoe that her brother, Walter, purchased from Native Americans in northern Wisconsin. The Menominee used similar canoes to travel across the Chain o' Lakes, strewing tobacco on the water to appease their monsters of the underworld—the Horned Serpent, White Deer, Underground Panther, and the Great White Bear—in the hope that their canoes would not capsize. (Ruth Benn.)

In 1855, Thomas Miner of New York purchased 80 acres of land on the east side of Miner Lake (pictured), and a year later, his relative J.H. Miner settled on 10 acres west of the lake. J.H. Miner's son, Wesley, fell in love with Mary Beasley, whose father, Cornelius, owned land on Beasley Lake and Creek. Wesley Miner and Mary Beasley married in 1866. (WHS.)

Joshua Foster Dake moved to Fremont from Pennsylvania in 1853 with his wife, Marbury, and six children. During an excursion into the Chain o' Lakes area before 1860, he purchased 50 acres of land between Long and Dake Lakes and eventually built a house facing the lake (pictured) that would later bear his name. Three of his sons fought in the Civil War. (Kent Pegorsch.)

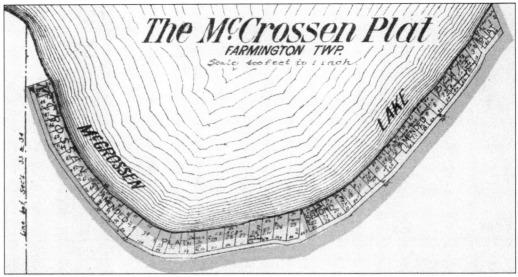

The McCrossen Plat
FARMINGTON TWP.
Scale 400 feet to 1 inch

John McCrossen, a New Brunswick native of Scots-Irish descent, migrated to the Town of Farmington from Maine with his family by 1860. He purchased land bordering the lake that now bears his name and farmed it until the 1890s, when he moved into the city of Waupaca. He died in 1904, leaving his lake property to his wife, Rachel, and daughters Carrie Felker and Mary Chady. By 1923, Carrie and Mary had subdivided all of the land along the lake's southern shore to sell to cottage builders, as shown in the above image. They kept most of their father's farmland, naming it the McCrossen Estate. The tourist in the image at left is posing with a "private property" sign on the estate. (Both, WHS.)

Two

FROM PIONEERS
TO PROPRIETORS

The businessmen and political leaders of Waupaca started to promote vacationing and tourism on the Chain o' Lakes in the 1880s to grow the population and economy in the area. Until the 1870s, Waupaca had only boasted a couple hundred residents who mainly farmed for subsistence and moved lumber camp supplies from Gill's Landing (near present-day Weyauwega) to Stevens Point. However, in the late 1860s, these community leaders set their sights on bringing a railroad to the community.

In February 1870, the Wisconsin Central Railroad surveyed Waupaca as a possible stop on a line between Menasha and Stevens Point. To assure that Waupaca would be chosen, area residents voted to give the Wisconsin Central $50,000 as an incentive, and the first train pulled into their settlement in September 1871. The railroad helped Waupaca to become a major supplier of potatoes, granite, and dairy products for the Midwest and nearly double its population by 1885.

Wisconsin Central also brought tourists to Waupaca. In the late 1870s, Waupaca locals started picnicking, camping, and fishing on the eastern shores of Rainbow Lake, and word of the Chain o' Lakes' beauty traveled around town. Waupaca leaders soon realized the potential of the lakes serving as a tourism destination and sought to attract the huge population of middle-class people across the country who began vacationing after the Civil War.

Waupaca's leaders played a huge role in building the Chain's tourism industry in the 1880s by marketing the natural beauty of the lakes, building vacation facilities, and attracting the Wisconsin Department of the Grand Army of the Republic to build the Wisconsin Veterans Home on Rainbow Lake in 1887. Waupaca became the gateway that visitors passed through to reach the lakes, and its residents became the greeters.

Early visitors to the Chain o' Lakes christened the beautiful lakes with their unique name. In an 1880 article for a Chicago newspaper, Waupaca lawyer Irving Lord encouraged tourists to visit "the already somewhat famous 'Chain o' Lakes.'"

On September 28, 1871, a large crowd gathered to watch the first Wisconsin Central Railroad locomotive pull into Waupaca; it was a 35-ton Baldwin engine called the Menasha (a similar locomotive is shown here). The engine left from Menasha, and when it passed Weyauwega, the engineer started pulling the whistle. The crowd in Waupaca became so excited that a few fistfights broke out. (Wisconsin Historical Society, WHS-131904.)

As the railroad brought more business to Waupaca in the 1870s, the Wisconsin Central built a large, two-story depot for the town in 1881. The building had a ticket office, waiting room, dining room, and hotel rooms but stopped lodging and feeding guests in 1886 after food service became available on the trains. The depot burned down in May 1907. (WHS.)

Lawyer Irving Lord became the first Waupaca resident to market the Chain o' Lakes as a tourist destination in the 1880s. Lord wrote several articles for newspapers in Milwaukee and Chicago describing the natural beauty and recreational appeal of the lakes with the hopes of attracting tourists, investors, and new residents to his hometown. He also spread word about the lakes through his professional and personal social network that spanned the country. (WHS.)

In the early 1880s, Waupaca residents greatly enjoyed exploring the three islands in the upper Chain o' Lakes. The Waupaca Rowing Club, a group of local businessmen who rowed on the lakes every summer, claimed the smallest island, which was then called Crescent because of its shape. The club built a rustic house on the island by 1883, and lake-goers dubbed it "Club Island." (WHS.)

In 1881, a group of Waupaca businessmen built a spacious house on the eastern shore of Rainbow Lake where they could spend summers with their families and friends. However, they changed their minds and opened the building as the Greenwood Park Hotel that summer. The businessmen managed the hotel with the aim of making guests "feel as though they were in a good, quiet home," renting rooms and private cottages to guests. Over the next three years, the hotel became so popular among vacationers that the Wisconsin Central Railroad considered buying it. However, the hotel's owners did not make enough money to cover their operation costs and closed the hotel after the summer of 1884. (Both, WHS.)

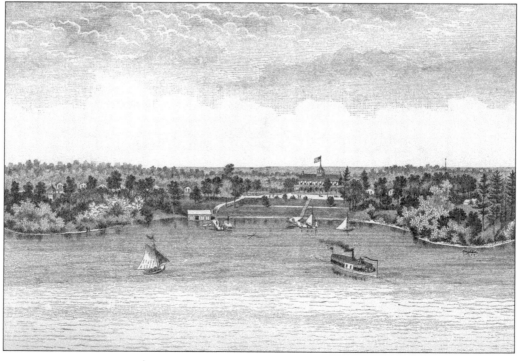

When his job as a Waupaca physician began harming his health, Dr. George Calkins purchased land on Sunset Lake in 1880 in order to spend summers there with his family. Two years later, Calkins discovered several springs on his property that yielded cold and clear water. He sent a sample of the water to Milwaukee chemist Gustavus Bode, who tested it and confirmed that the water was rich in minerals and free from the organic matter often found in fresh water. (WHS.)

Dr. George Calkins built a spring house (pictured) and factory to bottle the spring water and started selling it nationwide in 1885, earning $3,000 in his first year. He marketed the water as a medicinal aid for ailments such as indigestion, constipation, diabetes, kidney stones, various urinary issues, edema, nervousness, and even tuberculosis. He named his business Shealtiel Mineral Springs after the Hebrew word meaning "asked of God." (WHS.)

Dr. George Calkins also hired a man to use Shealtiel Mineral Springs water to make soft drinks such as ginger ale and birch beer. Calkins sold the drinks with ice cream at a stand on his property, Lake Park, and young people from the area began picnicking and socializing there throughout the day and evening. This photograph shows people relaxing at Lake Park around 1900. (WHS.)

In 1881, David Taylor built a large stone house on the banks of Taylor Lake (shown here around 1930) and operated it as a hotel for tourists. Mound Grove, a collection of around 15 Native American effigy mounds, surrounded the house. Taylor also owned a beautiful grove on Taylor Lake's north shore that was used by a Methodist church in Waupaca for annual camp meetings. (WHS.)

MARDEN HALL, WISCONSIN VETERANS' HOME, WAUPACA, WIS.

In February 1887, the Wisconsin Department of the Grand Army of the Republic (GAR) resolved to found a retirement home for Civil War veterans and their wives, as well as war widows. The City of Waupaca persuaded GAR officials to locate the home on the former grounds of the Greenwood Park Hotel on Rainbow Lake by purchasing the site and donating it to the GAR. The GAR renamed the hotel building Marden Hall. (WHS.)

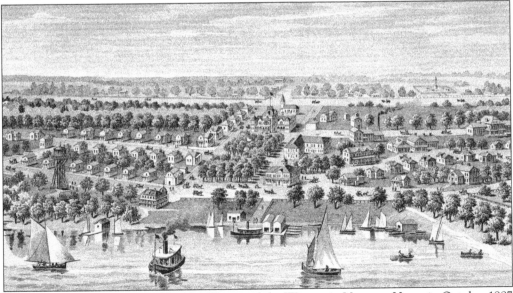

The Grand Army of the Republic (GAR) opened the Wisconsin Veterans Home in October 1887 and constructed several additional buildings by 1893 (the date of this image), including a hospital, a dining hall, and a few dormitories. Many GAR posts, individuals, businesses, and charitable organizations donated the money to build around 40 cottages for Civil War veterans and their wives to live in together. (WHS.)

21

On August 29, 1888, around 6,000 people from all over the state excitedly attended the formal dedication of the Wisconsin Veterans Home. Leaders of the Grand Army of the Republic spoke, and several Waupaca music groups performed, including the Smith brothers' brass band. All four of the brothers later joined the Veterans Home Cornet Band pictured here around 1890. (WHS.)

The Grand Army of the Republic (GAR) incorporated elements of military life into the Wisconsin Veterans Home, including requiring residents to wear uniforms and giving staff members military job titles. The superintendent of the home was called "Commandant," and the GAR built a beautiful Queen Anne house (pictured) in 1888 for him to live and work in. William Waters, a popular Oshkosh architect, designed the structure. (WHS.)

Photographer H.H. Bennett of the Wisconsin Dells took this photograph of 21st Wisconsin Infantry Regiment veterans and their wives posing in front of their building at the Wisconsin Veterans Home during the 1890s. The regiment constructed the building in 1894 as a dormitory for their aging members. Hundreds of people visited the Wisconsin Veterans Home to see friends and family, attend reunions and special events, inspect the cottages they maintained, and admire the patriotic institution that took such good care of aging Civil War veterans and their wives, as well as war widows. These visitors spread the word of the area's beauty and local attractions, fueling the tourism industry surrounding the Chain o' Lakes. (Wisconsin Historical Society, WHS-83779.)

Early visitors had to travel from the Wisconsin Central depot in Waupaca to the Wisconsin Veterans Home in horse-drawn carriages, like the one Clarence and Fannie Bemis of Dayton and their children (shown here) used during a visit in 1900. Clarence's father, Levi Bemis, served in the 12th Wisconsin Infantry Regiment during the Civil War and most likely lived at the home at this time. (WHS.)

By 1890, the Wisconsin Veterans Home had purchased Maple Island, the largest island in the Chain o' Lakes located north of the home, for its residents to use as a park. It was renamed Home Island. After William H. Lent of Green Bay and his wife, Sarah, moved to the home by 1905, they began camping on the eastern end of the island, as shown on this postcard. (WHS.)

Three

FORGING A
VACATION COMMUNITY

From 1890 to 1920, the Chain o' Lakes boomed as a vacation destination, attracting tourists from all over the country. In 1907, the *Waupaca Record* reported that over 20,000 people had visited the lakes that summer, projecting that "with continued effort there is no reason why Waupaca should not lead the summer resorts of the Northwest."

The reason for this rise in popularity was that families who lived on the Chain o' Lakes, Waupaca businessmen, and outside organizations built and created a diverse array of lodging facilities and attractions that appealed to a variety of tourists. Traditional vacationers who just wanted to escape their everyday lives and relax could stay at rustic hotels, like Locksley Hall on Round Lake and the Brinsmere Inn on Sunset Lake, or the fashionable Grand View Hotel on Rainbow Lake.

Several outside groups created vacation spots on the lakes where tourists could educate their minds and exercise their bodies. The Roman Catholic Society of Jesus built the Loyola Villa on the northeast shore of Rainbow Lake in 1896 as a religious retreat where Jesuit priests and teachers could reconnect with their faith. A year later, the Wisconsin lodge of the International Order of Good Templars founded Camp Cleghorn on Columbia Lake, offering annual assemblies that blended the characteristics of educational Chautauqua gatherings and religious camp meetings. The Boys' Brigade of Neenah started a camp on Onaway Island in 1911 for its young members to build leadership skills and moral character in the wilderness.

To make travel from Waupaca to the Chain o' Lakes easier and quicker, the Waupaca Electric Light Association constructed a trolley line that transported tourists from the Wisconsin Central Railroad depot to the Wisconsin Veterans Home and Grand View Hotel. Residents who lived on the Chain built and operated steamboats that took tourists around the lakes and transported visitors from the Grand View Hotel to other hotels and attractions.

Much like the prominent businessmen of the Gilded Age, Waupaca residents and outsiders forged a tourism industry on the beautiful lakes they adored.

William and Elizabeth Smith (both seated) settled on land north of Round Lake and west of Rainbow Lake in 1858 and raised four sons on their farm. In 1881, they started boarding tourists in their farmhouse after a Mrs. Andre begged William to let her and her family stay there. The Smiths quickly became popular hosts and gained such a large clientele that William built four guest cottages. (WHS.)

This photograph shows the four Smith boys: (seated, left to right) David, Fred, Alfred and (standing) Edwin. David farmed part of his parents' land, Fred ran the Brinsmere Inn, and Alfred worked for a milling company in Minneapolis. Edwin spent nine years in North Dakota learning to be a photographer before returning home to become the business manager of Locksley Hall—his family's inn—because of his parents' advanced age. (WHS.)

Fred Smith opened the Brinsmere Inn (pictured) on the west shore of Sunset Lake in the summer of 1892 with his wife, Minnie. The inn initially consisted of a main building and a freestanding dining hall (at right), but Minnie and Fred were such admired proprietors that they built four cottages, an office, and a sitting room by 1907, bringing their capacity to 80 guests. They closed the hotel in 1916. (WHS.)

After their farmhouse burned down in 1897, William and Elizabeth Smith decided to open a full-fledged rustic resort on the north shore of Round Lake. They constructed a building with 20 guest rooms and a separate dining hall, naming the inn Locksley Hall after Alfred Tennyson's poem of the same name. The Smiths operated the inn with a small staff and endeared hundreds of guests with their kind and intelligent personalities. (Author's collection.)

Locksley Hall's popularity pushed owners William and Elizabeth Smith to build nine guest cottages and an amusement hall, which allowed them to accommodate up to 125 guests at one time. After Elizabeth's death in 1911, William ran Locksley Hall for seven more years. Several owners tried to run the inn—under the new name Locksley Lodge—into the 1940s but never achieved the Smiths' level of success. (Kent Pegorsch.)

This photograph shows a Locksley Lodge visitor joyfully drinking water from the pump in 1925. Tourists loved staying at the rustic inns at the Chain o' Lakes because they received the full country experience: they ate meals made with farm-fresh ingredients, stayed in buildings without indoor plumbing or electricity, did not follow a strict schedule, and spent most of their time outdoors. (Kent Pegorsch.)

Vacations at Locksley Hall and Brinsmere Inn revolved around the piers at the two places of lodging. In addition to swimming, canoeing, and fishing, guests could ride William Smith's two steamboats, the *Queen* and *Lady of the Lake* (formerly named the *Sunrise*), or Fred Smith's steamboat, the *Brinsmere*, around the lakes. The Smiths were also the first proprietors on the Chain o' Lakes to offer organized Crystal River canoe trips. Fred and William provided guests with canoes and lunches, dropped them off at the mouth of the river in Long Lake, then picked them up in Parfreyville in the evening in a horse-drawn wagon. The above picture shows the Locksley Lodge pier in the 1920s, while the below picture shows a vacationer canoeing near the same pier in 1925. (Above, WHS; below, Kent Pegorsch.)

A group of Waupaca investors built the Grand View Hotel (pictured above) with 20 guest rooms and a dining hall just southwest of the Wisconsin Veterans Home on Rainbow Lake in 1894. The investors leased the property to two experienced hotel managers, Chris Hill of Shawano and Sam Nessling of Chicago, who successfully operated the hotel until 1899. There was such a high demand for guests that Hill and Nessling constructed the Annex building (pictured below) with 45 additional guest rooms. Irving Lord of Waupaca started leasing the Grand View Hotel in 1901 and bought it in 1904, running it in conjunction with his electric trolley business. (Above, Bob and Mary Ann Wells; below, WHS.)

THE
GRAND VIEW HOTEL
AND
COTTAGES.
WAUPAGA, WIS.

THE GRAND VIEW.

IDEAL FAMILY
RESORT

ON THE CHAIN O'LAKES

GRAND VIEW HOTEL CO.,
PROPRIETORS.
IRVING P. LORD, PRESIDENT.

THE ANNEX.

Proprietor Irving Lord envisioned the Grand View Hotel as a luxury resort for wealthy families. After purchasing the hotel in 1904, Lord updated the hotel's buildings and grounds with electric lights and began developing a diverse array of activities to appeal to people of all ages and interests. He later added indoor plumbing and other luxury amenities, mailing out annual brochures—like this one—to advertise changes. (Author's collection.)

The Grand View Hotel provided guests with first-rate amenities, including fine dining, daily bedroom-cleaning, on-call service, bathrooms, a swimming beach, sporting facilities, fishing instruction, rowboat rentals, weekly dances, and musical entertainment. The hotel employed many people to provide these services, as shown in this photograph of the 1904–1905 staff. (WHS.)

As this photograph of a Fourth of July meal in 1897 shows, dining at the Grand View Hotel was an extravagant affair. Hotel rules required guests to wear formal attire to dinner and servants and children to eat in a separate dining room. A team of chefs crafted delicious meals for guests exclusively using fresh ingredients from local farms. (WHS.)

Grand View Hotel guests who wanted more privacy could rent one of the hotel's 10 cottages, including the one pictured here. Each cottage had a living room with a fireplace, four sleeping rooms, a screened-in porch with a cot, and electric lights. Guests had to use bathrooms at the hotel and Annex but could press an electric bell to have hot or cold water delivered. (WHS.)

When it opened, the Grand View Hotel had a dock and boathouse where patrons could swim and take out small boats. The hotel's proprietor, Irving Lord, later expanded the boathouse, added a cigar and refreshment stand on the dock, built a bathhouse, and installed a toboggan slide. The bathing area (pictured) was in a shallow portion of Rainbow Lake. (Bob and Mary Ann Wells.)

This photograph shows a group of Grand View Hotel guests on top of a nearby hill eating a picnic lunch prepared by the hotel's kitchen. Guests loved exploring the surrounding landscape because it was covered with trees and plants, had various hills and slopes, and was dry. The hotel also offered guides for hire to show guests all the good fishing spots in the area. (WHS.)

The Society of Jesus, the Roman Catholic order of priests and brothers with members called Jesuits, purchased land on the northeastern shore of Rainbow Lake in 1895 after one of its members learned of the property while ministering at the Wisconsin Veterans Home. The following spring, the society built the Loyola Villa, a two-story structure with a wide veranda (pictured above), facing the water on top of the property's steep bluff. Teachers and professors from the society's high schools and colleges in the Midwest used the villa as a summer retreat until World War I (a group is pictured below in 1897). After the war, young men training to be Jesuits started staying and taking classes at the villa. (Both, Jesuit Archives & Research Center.)

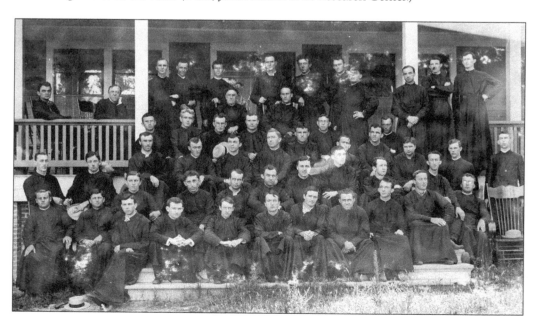

The Jesuit priests, brothers, and scholastics engaged in religious study and reflection while staying at Loyola Villa. In Roman Catholic tradition, the Jesuits built this shrine to the Virgin Mary in a grotto of rocks near the lakeshore where they could pray through her intercession. The fate of this shrine is unknown, but in 1904, the Jesuits built a similar shrine on the hillside that is still intact. (Jesuit Archives & Research Center.)

Loyola Villa was also a place where Jesuits could relax and rejuvenate their minds and bodies. They played softball and tennis, swam and boated around the Chain o' Lakes, rode horses, played instruments, and sang. The Jesuits became well-known on the lakes for the beautiful singing voices they shared with vacationers while rowing across the water. (Jesuit Archives & Research Center.)

The Wisconsin lodge of the International Order of Good Templars, an organization that advocated for temperance (the moderation of alcohol consumption), established a family campground for its members on the southern shore of Columbia Lake in 1897. Members named it Camp Cleghorn after Capt. John F. Cleghorn, who located the property and arranged the purchase of it. The Wisconsin lodge hosted annual two-week assemblies that provided religious meetings, wholesome entertainment, educational lectures on temperance, and recreational activities for Good Templars from across the Midwest. Famous speakers included orator and politician William Jennings Bryan and Wisconsin governor Robert LaFollette. For the first few decades, campers mostly stayed in cottage-sized tents like those shown above. Capt. Justin Wood, a founder of the camp, operated boats (shown below) that brought visitors directly to Camp Cleghorn from the Electric Dock. (Both, WHS.)

For most of the 20th century, Camp Cleghorn had a large dining hall and kitchen building (at left) where campers could eat every day, and the public could eat there on Sundays. A second-floor dormitory housed girls who served and cooked. The camp also had a store (at right) that sold almost everything campers might need, including produce, meats, baked goods, fresh milk, tents, hardware, camping equipment, and cleaning supplies. (Tom Charlesworth.)

The Good Templars constructed the tabernacle—a church/auditorium space—to host assembly lectures, concerts, and nondenominational church services. It originally had a sand floor, split-log benches for church pews, gaslights, and side doors that could be raised. Sometime in the 1970s, Camp Cleghorn residents renovated the barnlike building, and today, it is mainly used as a chapel. (Author's collection.)

In 1898, Irving Lord and W.B. Baker, owners of the Waupaca Electric Light Association, obtained permission from the City of Waupaca to build the Waupaca Electric Railway, a 4.5-mile trolley line connecting the Wisconsin Central depot in Waupaca with the Wisconsin Veterans Home and Grand View Hotel. Between May and July 1899, a Chicago construction company laid the line between the depot and the Wisconsin Veterans Home (the construction is shown above), and the first trolley ran on July 4 to the delight of onlooking locals. Lord and Baker purchased five used streetcars from Milwaukee to use on the tracks and powered the line with a dam on the Waupaca River and a coal-fired plant. Waupaca residents, including the conductor and motorman shown below, worked on the trolley. (Both, WHS.)

By July 21, 1899, laborers had finished laying the track for the Waupaca Electric Railway to its last stop on the grounds of the Grand View Hotel. Tourists could walk directly from this stop to the hotel's dock or the Electric Dock to catch a steamboat if they were staying somewhere else on the lakes. (WHS.)

The trolley's baggage car served the important function of moving tourists' trunks and other luggage from the Wisconsin Central depot to the Chain o' Lakes. The Waupaca Area Model Railroaders acquired the baggage car in 1992 and restored it. This photograph shows a tractor pulling the restored car in Waupaca's Fourth of July parade in 2000. (WHS.)

The Waupaca Electric Railway moved toward the Wisconsin Veterans Home along the road that is now County Highway QQ and stopped at a small depot (at left) near the intersection of King Street. The trolley was largely responsible for the development of the home's commercial district because the owners of local businesses, like the Home Grocery (at right), built along the railway to attract riders. (WHS.)

In 1900, Irving Lord and W.B. Baker purchased an enclosed winter car (shown here in 1916) with an electric heater from the Jewett Car Company based in Ohio. The Waupaca Electric Railway operated in the winter to deliver mail to the Wisconsin Veterans Home and provide a safe, warm way for people who lived at and around the home to travel to Waupaca. (WHS.)

After the old depot burned down in 1907, the Wisconsin Central quickly constructed a new depot that opened in 1908; it is shown here in the 1940s. To meet the needs of tourists coming through Waupaca, the depot had a large ticket office/operator's room, a general waiting room with a fireplace, a women's parlor with adjoining toilet rooms, a men's smoking room, and a hot water furnace. (WHS.)

Waupaca businessmen, backed by the city government and voters, incorporated the Waupaca Green Bay Railroad in 1907 and constructed nine miles of track from Waupaca northward to Scandinavia, connecting Waupaca with the Green Bay & Western Railroad. Businessmen wanted the railroad for economic reasons, but it also provided another way for tourists from central Wisconsin to travel to Waupaca. (WHS.)

In 1907, the Boys' Brigade of Neenah, a youth organization, held its annual camping trip on Columbia Lake. During the trip, campers discovered the overgrown Juniper Island between Sunset and Rainbow Lakes. The brigade arranged to camp there during the summers of 1908, 1910, and 1911, and the boys loved it so much that S.F. Shattuck, the brigade's captain, personally purchased the island for the organization in the fall of 1911. Three years later, the brigade formed an association to manage the island and renamed it Onaway after an Ojibwe Indian word interpreted as meaning "alert" or "awaken." Until the 1930s, the boys stayed in tents on the island, as shown in these images from the 1910s. (Above, WHS; below, BGB.)

Before the 1950s, members of the Boys' Brigade of Neenah spent one week at Camp Onaway in June. Camp leaders organized numerous activities for the boys, including swimming, sports, games, chapel services, rowing, canoeing, campfires, chores, and military-style dress parades. This picture from the 1910s shows a group of boys who won first place in one of the camp's many athletic competitions. (BGB.)

Camp Onaway participants spent time on the water daily. Boys had to demonstrate to camp leaders that they could swim in order to be able to use the pier, diving boards, and high-diving deck/chute slide (pictured here), but those who could not swim learned during lessons. The boys also fished, crafted and floated small sailboats, raced in long rowboats, and canoed down the Crystal River. (BGB.)

James P. Mallette, a wealthy real estate businessman from Chicago, purchased land on the southern peninsula between Round and McCrossen Lakes around 1896 and built a cottage called Fern Terrace facing Round Lake. James's wife, Mabel, and their seven children spent summers there, with James most likely visiting on weekends. After James's untimely death in 1903 at age 43, Mabel inherited Fern Terrace and continued vacationing there with her children until she sold it by 1923. Mabel occasionally rented out the cottage, as was the case in this 1921 photograph that was taken when Nathan Cohen, owner of the Fair Store in Waupaca, hosted all of his employees at the cottage after he sold the store. (WHS.)

Four

RISE OF A COTTAGE CULTURE

Starting in 1900, tourists visiting the Chain o' Lakes slowly began to prefer staying in cottages instead of the old hotels and inns. Cottages offered more privacy, direct contact with nature, and freedom from hotels' strict schedules, which appealed to a new generation of vacationers who wanted to explore the countryside in automobiles, the new mode of transportation taking over the United States.

Waupaca-area locals and tourists had been staying in cottages since the Chain o' Lakes first became a vacation destination in the 1880s. The Greenwood Park Hotel, Grand View Hotel, and the Smiths' inns all offered private cottages for their guests. Waupaca locals had also built their own private cottages on the lakes for weekend jaunts.

In the 1890s, a few residents began subdividing their Chain o' Lakes properties to sell as individual lots, often working with builders to construct cottages on them. Volney Calkins, the owner of a farm that stretched from McCrossen Lake to what is now Wisconsin Highway 54, platted the first cottage subdivision on the lakes, Point Comfort, on the western shore of Rainbow Lake by 1889. Over the next 34 years, local landowners platted 12 more subdivisions on the Chain o' Lakes, and this trend increased in popularity for the rest of the century until most of the lakes' shores were filled with individual properties.

Many families built or bought their own cottages that they stayed at every summer or rented locals' cottages. While staying at these cottages, families had to complete all of their housekeeping, cook their own meals, and entertain themselves. The cottages also lacked modern amenities and could only be lived in during the summer. Despite this, families cherished their cottages and often gave them unique names.

Cottages quickly became the best places to stay at the Chain o' Lakes because they were more personal, family-focused, and memorable than the Grand View Hotel and the Smiths' inns. The cherished memories families made at their cottages over multiple generations have undoubtedly allowed the lakes to continue flourishing as a vacation destination up to the present day.

By 1896, Charles Eseman, a photographer from Waupaca, built the Crow's Nest cottage (pictured) on the southwestern shore of Sunset Lake. E. Griffith Williams, a businessman from the Chicago area, purchased the cottage by 1927 and spent summers with his family there until 1945. Williams established the Riverside Golf Course in Waupaca in 1937. (WHS.)

Thomas Hyde, a Stevens Point insurance salesman, built the Hyde Park cottage at the end of Highland Lane by 1896. He later moved the cottage to the western point of Sunset and Rainbow Lakes during a winter around 1900, placing the structure on logs and employing horses to pull it. Thomas Hyde's daughters, Amy Ann Oster and Sarah Elizabeth Shumway, owned the cottage until the late 1930s. (Bob and Mary Ann Wells.)

Rev. Enoch Perry and his wife, Sarah, who are pictured below, began vacationing on the Chain o' Lakes in 1891 while he was the pastor of First United Methodist Church in Waupaca. In 1901, the couple purchased a cottage (pictured above) in the Point Comfort subdivision on Rainbow Lake, naming it Newdale Cottage after their hometown in Shropshire, England. Enoch and Sarah vacationed at the cottage with their children—and, eventually, grandchildren—until their respective deaths in 1953 and 1948. During that time, they greatly improved the cottage, adding three upstairs rooms in 1924, indoor plumbing in 1925, and a refrigerator and water heater in 1940. Enoch and Sarah's daughter Eva Perry owned Newdale Cottage from 1953 until her death in 1962 and left the cottage to her niece, Dorothy Krueger, whose descendants still stay at the cottage today. (Above, WHS; below, Newdale Cottage Archive.)

In 1900, Edward E. Browne, a Waupaca lawyer and Republican politician, purchased a large lakefront property stretching from the eastern shore of Round Lake to the western shore of Nessling Lake. Edward built his cottage, Summertime, on Round Lake, and it became his refuge when he served in the Wisconsin State Senate from 1907 to 1912 and in the US House of Representatives from 1913 to 1931. Like his Chain o' Lakes neighbor Sen. George W. Norris, Edward Browne supported progressive legislation and championed the rights of the working class. The below photograph shows members of the Browne family posing near Summertime. They are, from left to right, Edward; Rose, his wife; Josie, his relative; Tom, his son; Jennie, his sister; and Clarence H. Truesdell, his brother-in-law. (Both, WHS.)

Edward E. Browne maintained much of his lakefront property on McCrossen Lake as a nature preserve known as Greenwood Forest (shown above). He established a small park east of his Summertime cottage and built a few small cottages on McCrossen Lake, which he gave to his teenage daughters, Katherine and Helen, and his brother-in-law, Clarence H. Truesdell. He subdivided and sold the land on the western shore of Nessling Lake to cottage-builders. Browne was an avid protector of natural areas and served on the Wisconsin State Conservation Commission from 1936 to 1941. The below photograph shows Edward in his later years in front of the garden house on his Greenwood Forest property with his wife, Rose; four children; one daughter-in-law; and five grandchildren. (Both, WHS.)

These photographs from around 1908 show members of the Blue Gill Club, a group of Waupaca men who went on annual trips filled with fishing, hunting, and drunken foolishness. The group's leader was John Ekstrom, a painter from Waupaca who started the business that became Nelson Painting Company. Ekstrom was a Swedish immigrant who married Matilda Hansen, a Danish immigrant, so the club may have been connected to the Danes' Home Society of Waupaca. The Blue Gill Club stayed at Albert Lund's cottage (shown below) on the western shore of Rainbow Lake in 1908. Lund, a Danish man, often rented out his cottage to tourists. (Both, WHS.)

Clarence H. Truesdell built a cottage named The Birches (shown above) on the eastern shore of McCrossen Lake by 1911. He was a successful pharmacist in Chicago before moving to Waupaca in 1894 and starting the business that later became the Stratton Drug Store. Clarence and his wife, Jennie Browne, loved spending summers at the cottage with their two children, Mary and Phillip (shown in the boat below), and often entertained members of their large extended family. After Clarence passed away from diabetes in 1917 at the age of 50, Jennie continued to stay at the cottage with her children—and, eventually, grandchildren—until the 1940s. (Both, WHS.)

In 1915, an unidentified family took these photographs while staying at the cottage owned by Belle Barnum Chamberlain of Waupaca on the northwestern shore of Columbia Lake. Chamberlain built this large two-story cottage by 1906 and owned it until her death in 1939, often renting it to vacationers. She led an active social life in Waupaca, participating in the Monday Night Club and serving on the Waupaca Library Board. The family who took these photographs spent their vacation exploring the Chain o' Lakes by canoe and gasoline launch. They also took great delight in the forested landscape around the Chamberlain cottage and the local wildlife, as evidenced in their interactions with a pheasant (shown below). (Both, Kent Pegorsch.)

Staying at a private cottage required vacationers to cook and clean for themselves and often isolated them from other tourists. However, many enjoyed this because it forced them to spend quality time with family and friends and enjoy the outdoors. This unidentified family found great delight in eating fresh watermelon while staying at the Chamberlain cottage in 1915. (Kent Pegorsch.)

The unidentified family traveled to the Chamberlain cottage in their trusty Ford Model T. Many vacationers began to prefer taking cars to the Chain o' Lakes in the 1910s because they did not have to follow a train schedule, give their luggage to porters, or spend extra time traveling from Waupaca to the lakes via the trolley. (Kent Pegorsch.)

George W. Norris (pictured at left) was a progressive Republican US senator from Nebraska who served from 1913 to 1943, passing major bills that included the 20th amendment and the 1932 Norris–LaGuardia Act. He recuperated from his work at the Chain o' Lakes, first staying at the Grand View Hotel around 1900 with his college friends, the Loyal United Nine (LUN) Club, for their annual banquets. In 1903, the group bought their own cottage, located in the Point Comfort subdivision on Rainbow Lake, for their reunions, but it soon grew too crowded. In 1920, George and his wife, Ellie, built their own cottage at Point Comfort named Haleiwa (pictured below in 1940) and stayed there almost every summer until he died in 1944. (Left, History Nebraska, RG3298.PH3-3; below, History Nebraska, RG3298.PH21-28.)

These photographs show a group of young adults, most likely high school or college students, posing in front of the Shady Beach cottage on Nessling Lake, probably in the 1920s. Bessie Nelsen of the Nelsen Boat Line and Cottages had built the cottage in 1906 using odds and ends and eventually added 11 additional rental cottages to her business. As the above photograph suggests, the cottages were simple structures adorned with fun, almost kitschy decorations. This group of young adults spent their time at the Chain o' Lakes swimming, exploring the nearby farmland, canoeing around the lakes, singing and playing instruments, and riding a gasoline launch. A few men and women chaperoned the young people to assure the trip was respectable. (Both, WHS.)

The shores of Long Lake, the southernmost lake of the Chain o' Lakes, remained largely free of tourists and buildings during the 20th century, making it the perfect lake for camping and staying in secluded cottages. The 1940s postcard above shows Long Lake's tree-covered western shore. Margaret Ashmun (pictured below around 1900), a writer from Rural, grew up visiting her family's cottage on the eastern shore of Long Lake and set her 1924 novel *The Lake* in a rural landscape inspired by the Chain o' Lakes area. The novel, a psychological drama, depicts a boy's relationships with his abusive father, secretive mother, and a mysterious neighbor who treats him like a son. (Above, Bob and Mary Ann Wells; below, Ruth Benn.)

In 1918, Katherine Beelen of Appleton stayed in a rental cottage on the eastern shore of Long Lake with her friend's family and loved it so much that she rented the neighboring cottage (shown above) for several summers. She purchased it in 1925 and married Arnold Laudert the following year. The below photograph depicts Katherine (center) swimming at the nearby Camp Cleghorn beach in 1928. Katherine and Arnold vacationed at their cottage with their two daughters and many grandchildren until their respective deaths in 1992 and 1982. The couple kept the cottage in its rustic state at the request of their children, but in 1991, their daughter, Rose Mary Rupnow, rebuilt the cottage on its original footprint. (Both, WHS.)

From the beginning, Camp Cleghorn vacationers who did not want to stay in tents built private cottages on lots leased from the camp. Until the 1930s, cottage-owners had to rent their structures during annual assemblies and give half of the earnings to the camp. Eventually, campers built a total of 42 cottages along the lakeshore, and cottage-owners became the main shareholders in the Camp Cleghorn organization. Previously, anyone who wanted to support the camp's temperance mission could buy stock. The above photograph shows a row of the camp's two-story cottages in the 1940s. The below photograph shows siblings Betty and Art Charlesworth posing on the camp's dock in front of a few one-story cottages in 1928. (Above, WHS; below, Tom Charlesworth.)

The Wisconsin Good Templars continued holding annual assemblies at Camp Cleghorn until the late 1940s but also hosted outside groups starting in the 1920s. Various church, youth, and nonprofit organizations, including the Walther League and Presbyterian Synod, held summer camps and events at the camp. This photograph shows Wisconsin Junior Chamber of Commerce members waiting for a launch during their annual picnic at Camp Cleghorn in 1935. (WHS.)

The Camp Cleghorn Store (shown in the 1940s) was a popular socialization area for campers from its construction in the camp's early years until its demolition near the end of the 20th century. Adults and children loved the convenience of being able to purchase candies, ice cream, and soda—in addition to necessities such as matches, firewood, staple foods, and automobile fuel—at a location so close to their cottages or campsites. (Jack Bonnell, Skip Bonnell, and Kristi Diaz.)

In 1929, Herman Cushman, the retired owner of a chain store in the Chicago area, built an elaborate summer home named Strongwood Cabin on the western point between Nessling and McCrossen Lakes. Designed by William Sandell of Barrington, Illinois, the cabin was entirely constructed of wood. The upstairs included three bedrooms and a library, and the downstairs included a living room with an eight-foot fireplace, dining room, bathroom, kitchen, breakfast room, and two bedrooms. Cushman only stayed at Strongwood Cabin for two years before he had a stroke and passed away there. Gerda Anderson, his live-in servant of 12 years, owned the cabin from 1932 until her death in the 1970s, and it is still in use today. The above photograph shows Strongwood Cabin in the 1930s, and the below one shows the cabin in the 1980s. (Both, WHS.)

Frank Hoaglin (pictured at right), owner of a Waupaca manufacturing company that produced flyswatters and no-spill gasoline funnels, built a few rustic cottages on the eastern shore of Sunset Lake by 1930 that he used himself and also rented out to tourists. In 1931, Dr. Paul Hodges (pictured below) of Chicago stayed at one of Hoaglin's cottages with his wife, Merle, and five children. Hodges was the chief of radiology at the University of Chicago and had visited the Chain o' Lakes a few times as a child because his mother grew up near Waupaca. In 1932, Hoaglin built Hodges a two-story log cottage named Longwood as well as a one-story building, called Shortwood, where Hodges could work. (Right, WHS; below, Special Collections Research Center, University of Chicago Library.)

The most famous cottage-dweller on the Chain o' Lakes was Esther Williams, a professional swimmer who became a celebrity after starring in aqua-musical movies during the 1940s. While married to radio singer Ben Gage from 1945 to 1959, she made a few visits to Club Island to stay at the cottage (shown here) owned by Gage's family. Many longtime residents and vacationers witnessed Williams swimming in Rainbow Lake, and local newspapers reported on her visits. Because of this, locals began calling the island "Esther Williams Island," and the name has stuck until the present day. The cottage on the island burned in a fire in 1950, and Williams and Gage sold the island to Hobert Edmunds, of Edmunds' Dock and Boat Line, in 1955. After Edmunds's death in 1963, his son, Don, rented—and later sold—the island to Camp Onaway. (WHS.)

From 1902 until at least 1941, Amelia Merriam (shown at right) operated a general store on the eastern shore of McCrossen Lake, mostly by herself. She called her business Lake Palace Grocery by the 1930s and operated the store on a dock (at left in the below image) so boaters could easily park to shop. She also may have made deliveries on her boat, the *Alice R.* Cottage vacationers and residents who had to cook their own meals must have greatly appreciated her business, as it saved them from having to make a trip into Waupaca. Amelia Merriam also rented out four cottages on McCrossen Lake and helped her husband, Charles, and daughter, Bessie, run the family's boat livery business. She retired around the age of 80. (Right, Jack Bonnell, Skip Bonnell, and Kristi Diaz; below, WHS.)

The US Postal Service started a marine mail route on the Chain o' Lakes in 1920 thanks to the efforts of Rep. Edward E. Browne. Until the mid-1970s, the postmaster at the Wisconsin Veterans Home contracted with a local man on a yearly basis to deliver mail via boat to cottages on the lakes in the summer. Cottage-dwellers only needed to place a mailbox on the edge of their pier to participate. The photograph at left shows two mailboxes on Newdale Cottage's pier in the 1950s. The longest-serving marine mail carriers at the lakes were Edwin Smith, who delivered mail in his checkerboard boat (pictured below) from 1922 to 1933, and Alfred Brandt, who served from 1935 to 1963. (Left, Newdale Cottage Archive; below, Kent Pegorsch.)

Five

ARE WE THERE YET?

Although cottages eventually became tourists' favorite places to stay on the Chain o' Lakes in the 20th century, they were not responsible for the decline of hotels and inns. The true culprit was the automobile and the impact it had on the tourism industry. Instead of following the schedules of railroads and hotels, automobile tourists wanted to travel at their own paces, explore the wilderness, and stop at unique places en route to their main destinations.

Chain o' Lakes tourists began coming to the area in automobiles during the late 1910s but were frustrated at the lack of hotels that rented rooms by the night instead of by the week, roadside attractions, and eateries. In response, area locals founded the Pines Inn and Fern Terrace, two wildly popular motor resorts, in addition to themed restaurants, entertainment venues, and other activities.

Without a doubt, the most popular of these new businesses were the Indian Crossing Casino on Columbia Lake and Whispering Pines Park on Marl Lake. Built in 1925 as a dance hall, the Indian Crossing Casino served as a prominent dancing and concert venue in Wisconsin through 1975, hosting famous entertainers such as Louis Armstrong and the Beach Boys. Whispering Pines Park delighted thousands of visitors each summer between the early 1930s and 1975 with its beautiful natural scenery, picnic grounds, and themed attractions.

The massive growth of family tourism in the United States in the 1950s influenced the residents of vacation spots to develop businesses that would entice traveling families. Chain o' Lakes residents followed suit, opening restaurants, gift shops, motels, and amusement parks in addition to modernizing older recreational facilities. The spirit of the first automobile tourists lives on today as tourists look for adventure in every corner of the Chain o' Lakes area.

This 1925 photograph shows a group of tourists posing with their automobile at Locksley Lodge. Fred Smith believed that automobiles caused the decline of rustic hotels like Locksley Lodge and Brinsmere Inn. In the late 1940s, Smith reminisced that automobiles encouraged many vacationers to take road trips instead of visiting a single location. This led tourists to stay at inns for a few nights and not always remember to show respect to their hosts. (Kent Pegorsch.)

The popularization of automobiles in the 1910s allowed tourists to directly travel to the Chain o' Lakes from their homes and travel between their hotels or cottages and downtown Waupaca. This led to a decline in ticket sales on the Waupaca Electric Railway starting in 1916, the same year Irving Lord sold the railway. On July 4, 1925, the railway's new owners ended services, and they removed the tracks shortly afterward. (WHS.)

A year after closing the Brinsmere Inn in 1916, Minnie Smith opened a new hotel called the Pines Inn (shown above on McCrossen Lake. She started out with just one large cottage, but the inn became so popular that she built a three-story lodge next to the cottage in 1920 and added a separate dining room and kitchen building in 1922. The lodge had a living room with a fireplace, a long screened-in porch, and eight guest rooms on two floors. After Minnie's death in 1943, her son Edwin Smith and his wife, Winnie, ran the Pines Inn until 1960, when Winnie passed away. Edwin also worked as the postmaster of the Wisconsin Veterans Home from 1934 to 1963. (Both, WHS.)

PINES INN - McCROSSEN LAKE
CHAIN O' LAKES - WAUPACA, WIS.

The Pines Inn had a large dining hall (shown here in the 1960s) with a great view of McCrossen Lake. Although the hall was mainly for guests, the Pines Inn hosted dinners and meetings for many organizations from central Wisconsin (including the Waupaca Lions Club) and private individuals, which brought in much-needed income and word-of-mouth advertisement. (Elmer and Sandy Keil.)

The Smiths, who owned the Pines Inn, made the inn friendly to motorists by laying out a dirt road on which guests could drive directly to the main lodge, small lodge (the 1917 cottage), dining hall, and cottage (built later). The small lodge had eight rooms on two floors, and the cottage had four rooms on one floor. (Elmer and Sandy Keil.)

James LaSage and his son James LaSage Jr. owned the Pines Inn from 1960 to 1962 before selling it to Otto and Genevieve Keil, who moved from Franklin Park, Illinois, with their son, Elmer, and three daughters—Sandra, Nancy, and Janice—to operate the inn. These photographs show how the Keils furnished the lounge in the main lodge (above) and the guest rooms in all of the buildings (below). The Keils opened the dining hall to the public, serving two large meals at breakfast and dinner in addition to a light lunch. They also offered laundry services, gave boat rides, and rented out canoes and motorboats to guests. The daughters took turns waitressing, cleaning guest rooms, and doing laundry, while Elmer washed dishes, maintained the boats and motors, and fueled and repaired portable heaters for the rooms. (Both, Elmer and Sandy Keil.)

The Keils maintained the buildings of the Pines Inn for the first five years they owned it. In 1967, they completely renovated the main lodge (pictured) and dining hall, removing the second story and the lake-facing section of the lodge, connecting the two structures, and completely changing the layout. The resulting building had four units—each with a kitchen, living room, bathroom, and two bedrooms—that the Keils rented out separately. Between two of the units was a coffee shop. The family stopped renting out the small lodge and cottage, instead turning them into residences. In the early 1970s, Otto and Genevieve Keil split the four units and other buildings between their son Elmer Keil and daughter Nancy Oftedahl. (Elmer and Sandy Keil.)

Fortunat F. Mann, a successful French chef who worked in Cincinnati, purchased the Fern Terrace cottage and surrounding property in 1924, opening it as a resort—with the same name—two years later. Guests could stay in the hotel's lodge (shown above) or one of eight cottages on a nightly or weekly basis and had access to the southern point between McCrossen and Round Lakes (shown below) for relaxation, boating, and swimming. Mann hired managers to operate Fern Terrace while he ran a restaurant in Indianapolis until 1934. He then directly managed the hotel and opened its dining room to the public, offering special Sunday meals of chicken and beef chops. After Mann's death in 1950, his wife, Clovis, and subsequent owners operated Fern Terrace until developers razed it to build the Wingspan condominiums in 1973. (Both, WHS.)

William R. Arnold of Chicago built a large dance pavilion and associated resort named the Indian Crossing Casino (pictured above) on the channel connecting Limekiln and Columbia Lakes in 1925. The casino included a 6,000-square-foot dance floor (shown below), a stage, restrooms, dressing rooms, a soda fountain, and a 400-car parking lot, while the resort offered rental cottages, a dock, toboggan slides, and a boat landing. Between 5,000 and 10,000 people attended the casino's grand opening on July 4, 1925, which included dances to the music of the Arabian Knights Broadcasting Orchestra of Chicago and numerous water contests. Arnold successfully ran the casino for four years, holding dances accompanied by big-band orchestras a few nights a week and all-day events on holidays. (Both, WHS.)

Paul Asplund and John Martin ran the Indian Crossing Casino jointly from 1930 until 1935, when John's son, Allen, bought out Asplund. Over the next 20 years, John and Allen Martin booked many famous acts that toured the Midwest, including big band leader Tiny Hill, burlesque entertainer Gypsy Rose Lee, and jazz musician Louis Armstrong. They also replaced the casino's original boat dock and deck on the Indian Crossing channel (shown above around 1930) with a beer bar and sun deck (shown below in 1961). From 1955 to 1960, James LaSage and his son, James LaSage Jr., former nightclub owners, operated the casino before selling to John Goeltzer, who booked several popular rock acts in the early 1960s, most notably the Everly Brothers and the Beach Boys. Goeltzer struggled to afford big-name entertainers as their rates got more expensive, and he closed the casino in 1975. (Both, WHS.)

After buying the Indian Crossing Casino in 1955, James LaSage and his son, James LaSage Jr., opened the Sugar Bowl, a small restaurant on the property that sold coffee, sandwiches, soft drinks, and ice cream. They also added an arcade room in the house adjacent to the casino. The Sugar Bowl building and house (shown here in August 1961) still stand today and serve as Ding's Dock's office and rental cottage, respectively. (WHS.)

In 1930, George and Leonora Scherbert of Stevens Point opened a barbecue pit shaped like a Dutch windmill and a restaurant called Dutch's Barbecue southwest of Edmunds' Dock and Boat Line on Taylor Lake. They added a dance hall in 1933 and renamed the restaurant The Windmill in 1934. The Scherberts (or a later owner) moved the restaurant farther northeast on what is now Highway QQ by 1940, and The Windmill remained open until the early 1970s. (WHS.)

By 1928, Harry and Anna Belle Sprauge of Green Bay had built and moved into an elaborate two-story house (shown above) on the southern shore of McCrossen Lake after Harry retired from his work at the Green Bay & Western Railroad due to illness. In 1929, the couple opened the Manitou Sandwich Shoppe in their lake house, selling drinks, ice cream, candy, tobacco, groceries, tapestries, and souvenirs. The Sprauges also hosted private gatherings with in-house musical entertainment and rented out rooms. A unique feature of the shop was its fireplace (shown below), which was built with stones from all 50 states. In 1932, Harry died of his illness at the age of 49; Anna Belle continued operating the sandwich shop through 1936. (Both, WHS.)

WINDMILL AND STONE STAIRWAY AT WHISPERING PINES
PARK ON MARL LAKE, WAUPACA, WIS.

GEORGE WASHINGTON'S PROFILE
WHISPERING PINES MARL LAKE WAUPACA

Whispering Pines Park began as the summer home of Christ and Emma Hyldgaard. In 1929, Christ sold his milk business in Chicago at the age of 42 due to his heart problems and purchased land covered in tall white pine trees on Marl Lake in the Little Chain. He and Emma transformed their undeveloped land into a relaxing estate, building a modern cottage, cobblestone pathways, and a stone stairway leading down to the lake with an adjacent Dutch windmill replica (shown above). Christ also built 43 birdhouses and assembled an impressive garden of uniquely shaped rocks from Waupaca County and Winchester Hill in England; these included rocks shaped like a bald eagle, Uncle Sam, and George Washington (shown at left). By 1932, the Hyldgaards were regularly welcoming tourists onto their property for free. (Both, WHS.)

Christ and Emma Hyldgaard's property, which they called Whispering Pines Park, became wildly popular as Christ and Emma regularly changed and added displays. In 1936, a total of 12,848 people visited from all over the United States and even a few foreign countries; in 1939, over 26,000 people visited. At the request of their guests, the Hyldgaards added a picnic grove (shown above) with tables and grills in 1935, a small stone refreshment stand (shown below) in 1939, and a small gift shop (later called the Annex) in 1940. By the late 1940s, the Hyldgaards had purchased most of the properties around Marl Lake; they used these to expand the park and rent out cottages. They never charged a general admission fee to visitors. (Both, WHS.)

Christ and Emma Hyldgaard valued suggestions and comments from visitors so highly that they set up a comments table, shown here around 1940. Almost every change and addition they made to Whispering Pines Park—from adding souvenir shops and refreshment stands to building or changing displays—started as a recommendation from a visitor. (WHS.)

All of Whispering Pines Park's outdoor displays were unique, witty, and memorable. Taking inspiration from nature, US history, and folklore, the Hyldgaards created a mailbox shaped like a covered wagon, a "Ye Old Wishing Well," a replica of an old mill moved by a pipe-fed trough, the Fountain of Youth (shown here), a glass box with stuffed squirrels playing cards, and many other exhibits. (WHS.)

BIRD HOUSES AND COVERED WAGONS AT WHISPERING PINES
MARL LAKE   WAUPACA, WIS.   E-2204

Marl Lake, a 21-acre lake with an emerald-green hue, greatly added to the natural beauty of Whispering Pines Park. By the water, the Hyldgaards built a T-shaped pier, a small viewing area with benches shaped like covered wagons, and a few birdhouses—designed like castles—for purple martins (all shown above). Visitors had to travel in small boats through the small lakes and shallow channels of the Little Chain to reach Marl Lake via water. The Hyldgaards also installed two vending machines on the pier that dispensed handfuls of oatmeal that guests could feed to the fish. Marl Lake had crystal-clear water, so guests could watch as fish gathered to eat the oatmeal flakes, as shown in the photograph at right depicting Christ Hyldgaard feeding fish with his hand. (Both, WHS.)

Whispering Pines Park boomed in the 1950s, bringing in over 78,000 visitors each summer. The biggest crowd in the park's history— 6,500 people—gathered on Sunday, July 11, 1954. To keep up with visitors, owners Christ and Emma Hyldgaard built a larger gift shop in 1951 that sold numerous branded souvenir merchandise, including pennants, toys, knickknacks, jewelry, cribbage boards, cedar boxes, Indian headdresses, moccasins, and other items. Visitors could also buy a variety of postcards ranging from basic snapshots of the park to ones with amusing text and pictures. Outside the shop were two correspondence tables where guests could fill out and mail postcards. The Hyldgaards also kept a can of peanuts behind the gift shop's counter to feed tame squirrels and chipmunks that wandered in. This 1955 photograph shows Christ Hyldgaard watching a squirrel inspect the register. (Wisconsin Historical Society, WHS-91821.)

In 1954, owners Christ and Emma Hyldgaard built a larger refreshment stand at Whispering Pines Park. The Hut (shown here) was located near the picnic area and sold beverages, candy, snacks, ice cream, hamburgers, hot dogs, and barbecue made using Emma's secret recipe. The old and new refreshment stands operated at the same time for many years. (WHS.)

The Hyldgaards constructed a playground at Whispering Pines Park in the 1940s that included swings, a large slide, teeter-totters, and a merry-go-round. By 1963, they had added fiberglass swings, a small slide, rodeo horses, and other equipment. This photograph shows the French siblings joyfully using the merry-go-round in the 1960s. (Debbie French-Wauters.)

In the 1940s, owners Christ and Emma Hyldgaard opened a small museum area at Whispering Pines Park to house numerous antiques and oddities they had collected or received as donations. The space soon became too small, so they constructed a museum building in 1955 that had tall wooden cases with lights and glass windows (shown above). The new museum contained rare clocks, vintage firearms and tools, stuffed animals, mounted fish, and other antiques. One memorable display included two stuffed white-tailed bucks with their antlers locked in combat (shown below). Even though it was dark and smelled musty, the museum was one of the most beloved attractions at Whispering Pines Park. (Above, the Byers family; below, Joel Jenswold.)

In August 1966, Christ Hyldgaard died of a heart attack—to the sorrow of everyone whose lives had been touched by Whispering Pines Park. His wife, Emma, continued operating the park with the help of their close friend from Chicago, Casey Nowicke, who worked as the full-time caretaker. Emma Hyldgaard passed away in January 1975, leaving Whispering Pines Park to the State of Wisconsin in her will under the condition that it remain a public park. That May, the land officially became part of the Hartman Creek State Park during a dedication ceremony (pictured). To the dismay of many locals and tourists, all the displays were sold, and the buildings and nonnatural features were demolished. Since its reopening in 1977, Whispering Pines Park has served the public as a beautiful natural area. (WHS.)

In the early 1930s, Ed Larkowski built a resort east of Whispering Pines Park on Pope Lake called Taddy Wawa. He decorated the lawns with quirky decorations, rock formations, and gardens (shown above) that were similar to those at Whispering Pines Park, but his main focus was renting out cozy cottages (shown below). By 1951, John Mahoksi, Taddy Wawa's new owner, had built a snack stand that sold hot dogs, hamburgers, chicken, and root beer (in frosted mugs) and opened a picnic area, likely to attract Whispering Pines Park visitors. After Taddy Wawa closed in the early 1960s, Christ and Emma Hyldgaard purchased the property but never developed it like the rest of their Whispering Pines Park. (Both, WHS.)

Lee Englebretson bought the Grand View Hotel in 1920 and ran it with moderate success. However, he struggled to attract automobile tourists, and the hotel's revenue plummeted during the Great Depression. After buying the hotel in 1938, Lee Yorkson immediately demolished the kitchen and servants' wings (shown here), and he got rid of the Annex in 1941. The State of Wisconsin purchased the property in 1945 and razed the remaining buildings a year later. (WHS.)

In 1941, the residents who lived at and around the Wisconsin Veterans Home successfully petitioned Congress through their representative, Reid F. Murray, to rename their post office after Gen. Charles King, a famous soldier and war writer who made Wisconsin home. Thus, the business and residential area around the home became known as King. This photograph shows King's Main Street (now called County Highway QQ) in the 1940s. (WHS.)

In 1949, Charles and Inez Batavia built the Siesta Motel, a collection of six cottages with two rooms each, at the junction of US Highway 10 and State Highway 54 northeast of the Chain o' Lakes. To attract families on road trips, the Batavias designed the motel with heating, private bathrooms, twin and double bedrooms, and private driveways. Subsequent owners kept the motel open until 1987. (WHS.)

The Indian Trading Post was a general store and gas station located on County Highway Q southeast of Indian Crossing from the late 1940s to the 1980s. It sold groceries, including meats and farm-fresh produce, in addition to ice cream, homemade fried cakes, and lunches. It was conveniently located for cottage-dwellers but eventually closed due to the establishment of bigger grocery stores closer to Waupaca. (WHS.)

The Wisconsin Veterans Home grew substantially in the 20th century, as it had to meet the needs of each new wave of veterans from the Spanish-American War, both world wars, and later wars. It has expanded from a capacity of 50 in 1887 to over 700 today. After partially funding the home since 1889, the State of Wisconsin completely took over its management in 1929. Travelers continued to visit the Wisconsin Veterans Home throughout the 20th century, which most likely influenced its administrators to build beautiful monuments and memorials to fallen soldiers. The home's cemetery—perhaps its greatest monument—was founded in 1888, and all men (and, starting in 1926, all women) who lived at the home had the option of being buried there with a headstone for free. This 1950s photograph by George Sroda of Amherst Junction shows a soldier playing "Taps" in the cemetery to honor the soldiers buried there. (WHS.)

By the 1950s, the Boys' Brigade of Neenah had transformed Onaway Island from a rustic hideaway to an established summer camp. The brigade built a mess hall (shown above in 1949) in 1915 and tents with wooden frames (shown below in 1954) in the 1930s. The tents had netting and canvas flaps that could be rolled down as siding. The brigade also wired the entire island with electricity by 1945, installed flush toilets in 1946, and added several other buildings and amenities. To help fund Camp Onaway, the Boys' Brigade of Neenah rented the space to male and female youth organizations and churches, but this failed to cover all the expenses, and the brigade deeded the camp to the Presbyterian Synod of Wisconsin in 1955. The synod struggled to maintain the camp and sold it back to the brigade in 1966. (Both, BGB.)

The Boys' Brigade of Neenah adapted the lakeshore on Onaway Island to make swimming and boating a safe and accessible activity for campers. By the 1950s, it had built a boathouse that could hold 15 vessels, a beach (shown above in 1956), an advanced swimming pier with a diving board (shown below in 1949), and a swimming raft on the northwestern shore of the island. The brigade also built a boat pier on the north shore, where Hobert Edmunds dropped off and picked up campers, and a beginner's swimming pier on the southeastern shore. Campers water-skied, rode around the lakes in motorboats, and learned to pilot paddleboats, kayaks, rowboats, and canoes. (Both, BGB.)

During the formative years at Camp Onaway, boys participated in camp activities individually, often avoiding activities they were not comfortable with. In 1937, four older boys in the brigade organized the campers into four groups named after Native American tribes—Menominee, Winnebago, Oneida, and Blackfeet. These groups competed against one another in games, athletic tournaments, swim meets, campfire programs, and tent and hygiene inspections (shown above). Under the new system, campers had to work together, and in the process, they gained new skills, participated more, and had a better overall camp experience. Camp Onaway has used the tribal system ever since. Early on, campers dressed in stereotypical Native American clothing and body paint for activities and ceremonies, as shown in the 1952 photograph below. (Both, BGB.)

After inheriting a cottage and large lot on Beasley and Bass Lakes in 1959, Greg Charlesworth, a schoolteacher from New London, built Tom Thumb Mini Golf. Charlesworth designed all 18 holes based on the hardest miniature golf holes he had played in the Midwest and constructed memorable hazards, or obstacles, for each one. The above photograph shows the windmill, paddleboat, rocking horse, and rocket hazards on the course. In 1973, two schoolteachers from Iowa named George and Jean Melby (pictured below at the castle hazard) purchased Tom Thumb and operated it during summertime for 30 years, first with the help of their young daughters LeAnn, June, and Carla and later by themselves. The Melbys and later owners did not make major changes to the miniature golf course, so it still retains its 1950s charm today. (Both, June Melby.)

In 1960, Delmar and Edna Schmidt, a retired couple, purchased the old Red Mill, a gristmill located southeast of the Chain o' Lakes on the Crystal River that operated from 1855 to 1959. The couple transformed the mill into a popular Colonial-themed shop (shown above) that sold antiques, furniture, and gifts. They worked with Sterling Schrock, a local historical builder, to construct and install a large reproduction of a 1700s American waterwheel (shown at left) between 1961 and 1963. An elevated chute dropped water on the wheel, causing it to turn four times every minute. The Schmidts also developed the land behind the mill into a beautiful park, adding a covered bridge across the Crystal River in 1970 and a small chapel in 1974. Their son, Don, took over the shop around 1990. (Both, WHS.)

Hartman Creek State Park opened in 1966 on land west of the Chain o' Lakes that George Allen had originally settled on in 1856. Allen and his son engaged in hop and dairy farming and built a farmhouse (shown above) in 1896. George's grandson, George W. Allen, inherited the farm in 1925 and turned it into a fish hatchery, creating several ponds by building dams on Hartman Creek, a tributary of Pope Lake. In 1939, the Wisconsin Conservation Department purchased the hatchery and operated it until 1960. The Wisconsin State Parks and Recreation Division then transformed the hatchery into a beautiful recreation area, laying out hiking trails, a group campground, and 35 family campsites (one is shown below). The state later added a swimming beach, 68 more campsites, and trails for snowmobiling and skiing. (Above, Wisconsin Historical Society, WHS-71336; below, author's collection.)

PONDEROSA AT CHAIN O' LAKES, WAUPACA, WISCONSIN

Joseph Koshnick of Stevens Point and his family opened a Wild West theme park named the Ponderosa in 1967. Located southwest of the intersection of State Highway 54 and County Highway QQ, the park included a frontier village with a blacksmith shop, jail, and saloon; an Indian village; a track for riding in antique model cars (pictured below in 1979); a swinging bridge; stagecoach rides; a miniature animal farm; a carousel; and a rideable model train (pictured above around 1970). Actors performed holdups, jailbreaks, and train robberies to the excitement of visitors. In 1973, Joe Leann purchased the Ponderosa, renaming it Fort Waupaca, and operated it through the summer of 1979. Developers later transformed the property into the Old Town Waupaca shopping village that opened in 1982. (Above, WHS; below, Joe and Ginny Leean.)

In 1978, Jeff Maiman, a 21-year-old chef from Waukegan, Illinois, opened the Wheelhouse Restaurant near Indian Crossing, introducing his famous pizza recipe and specialty Italian sausage sandwich, the Bomber, to the Chain o' Lakes area. The Wheelhouse building originally housed Bud and June Diley's home-style restaurant called the Hearth from 1947 to 1964, followed by a series of short-lived restaurants, including the Pizza Place, the Grill, and Terry Teske's Wheelhouse. Maiman expanded and extensively renovated the building before opening his Wheelhouse and later added a unique 38-foot outdoor deck designed like a sailboat. In 1986, Maiman bought the house next door and renovated it into an ice-cream parlor and arcade called Scoopers (pictured below). Both establishments remain favorites among tourists and locals. (Both, author's collection.)

In 1986, Robert Gruenenfelder, better known as Cheesie Bob, opened the Bleu Cheese House in an old house in King. Gruenenfelder worked as a cheesemaker, like his father and grandfather, for most of his adult life, then took jobs as a car salesman and spice-blender before he decided to start a business. He ran the Bleu Cheese House by himself for almost a decade, selling cheese, gifts, and eventually liquor. The above photograph from the 1990s shows him in the store. In 1988, an advertising salesperson came up with the idea of putting a photograph of Cheesie Bob's face on a mouse for advertising purposes, as shown on the billboard pictured below. In 2018, Cheesie Bob closed his business and retired. (Both, Cheesie Bob.)

Six

ONE AFTER ANOTHER

Despite the unique hotels, cottages, and businesses surrounding the Chain o' Lakes, the area's biggest attraction has always been the lakes themselves. Tourists and locals have long enjoyed exploring the lakes via boat to take in the beautiful scenery, swim in the crystal-clear water, catch the fish lurking beneath the waves, and spend time with others. At first, lake-goers only used canoes and rowboats, but as boating technology advanced in the 20th century, they began to utilize motorboats that became faster and more user-friendly with each passing year.

Starting in the 1870s, many local entrepreneurs built or commissioned steamboats to give tours of the Chain o' Lakes to paying customers. All of the tour boats fiercely competed with each other to capitalize on the crowds of tourists who began vacationing on the lakes in the 1880s and 1890s. Most tour-boat owners picked up their patrons on the few docks on Taylor and Rainbow Lakes that private individuals and the Wisconsin Veterans Home had built for public use.

The introduction of gasoline motors shortly after 1900 allowed the next generation of tour-boat operators—a few of whom were the children of those early Chain o' Lakes steamboat owners—to construct or purchase motorized launches that were smaller, quicker, and cheaper to operate and maintain. These new tour-boat operators built full-fledged boat liveries on the lakes in the 1920s that rented canoes, rowboats, and motorboats to tourists. In addition, they continued operating tour boats and offered organized canoe trips down the Crystal River, one of the oldest traditions at the Chain o' Lakes. Boat liveries adapted as it became more common for individuals to own motorboats, adding boat repair, boat sales, and fuel sales to their services.

The Chippewa Indians who traveled through Waupaca County called the Chain o' Lakes *Wai-wai-ba-si-pi*, meaning "soon one after another." Whether traveling by canoe, rowboat, steamboat, or motorboat, tourists and locals have eagerly traveled from lake to lake wondering what new experiences each one would bring.

Sometime in the 1870s or 1880s, Henry Mumbrue of Waupaca built the Chain o' Lakes' first steamboat, an unnamed sternwheeler, and hired a pilot to give tours of the lakes for 10¢. Several Waupaca businessmen soon followed, including Maj. R.N. Roberts, who purchased the *Sunrise* and *Queen* from Jim Jensen, a Waupaca boatbuilder, and hired a Wisconsin Veterans Home resident to pilot them. In the 1890s, a Mr. Jenny piloted the *Catamaran* (shown above), a flat-bottomed steamboat powered by an underwater propeller, and held concerts and dances on its deck. Steamboats moved very slowly, so passengers spent a lot of time enjoying the scenery and each other's company. The 1899 photograph below shows Nettie Carpenter (at center in the first row) and her friends having fun on a steamboat ride. (Both, WHS.)

The Indian Crossing channel that connects the upper and lower Chain o' Lakes has been a popular spot for recreational boaters since at least the 1880s. The channel was originally so shallow that Native Americans waded across it or used a simple log bridge, and pioneers built a basic wooden bridge with stone supports to easily cross the channel via carriage. Local investors, including hotel owners, paid to have the channel deepened and bridge raised higher in 1883 and again in 1894 to allow steamboats to pass. However, many steamboat captains still lowered their smokestacks to clear the bridge and occasionally got stuck in the channel. As this photograph from around 1905 shows, locals stuck pointed sticks in the channel to help boats avoid its shallow portions; these are not unlike the crayon-shaped buoys there today. Sometime in the 1920s, an all-concrete bridge with a large rectangular opening was built. (WHS.)

Traveling around the Chain o' Lakes in rowboats and early motorized boats before the 1920s was a drastically different experience than modern boating. Lake-goers wore formal clothes that included casual suits and top hats for men and ankle-length dresses and summer hats for women. Accidentally falling into the water would have been an unpleasant and possibly dangerous experience while wearing such heavy clothes. The above photograph shows Roy Chady (right) of Waupaca piloting his small motorized boat, the *Wanita*, with Nina and Nathan Lockney, his sister and brother-in-law, in the 1910s. The below photograph shows a group of tourists in a rowboat on Columbia Lake in 1915. (Above, the family of Herbert Wenberg; below, Kent Pegorsch.)

OUTLET YOUNG'S LAKE, CHAIN O'LAKES, WAUPACA, WIS.

Early tourists loved visiting the Little Chain, a group of eight small yet deep lakes connected by shallow channels in the southwestern part of the Chain o' Lakes. Developers did not reach these lakes until the late 1920s, so they remained enclosed with trees and native vegetation for longer than the other Chain o' Lakes. Tourists must have felt like they were traveling into a separate world as they entered Beasley Lake from Long Lake and then rowed down the long creeks to each new lake. The above postcard shows a couple rowing by an old walking bridge while traversing the channel between Youngs and Bass Lakes around 1909, while the below photograph shows a man preparing to hunt near Marl Lake around 1905. (Above, Elmer and Sandy Keil; below, WHS.)

MARL LAKE

Capt. Justin Wood of Waukesha operated a dock and boat livery at Camp Cleghorn from 1897 until his death in 1924. Wood operated several steamboats—and, later, motor passenger boats—to transport tourists from the Electric Dock to the camp and out on sightseeing tours. The above photograph shows a group of tourists on one of his gasoline-powered launches, the *Idle Hour*, in 1915. Wood also rented out canoes, rowboats, and fishing equipment. In the 1930s, Dave Sebora, whose family owned a cottage at Camp Cleghorn, operated the camp's livery out of the boathouse pictured below. Sebora was paralyzed from polio but loved swimming and boating and used a little red coaster wagon to move around the boathouse. (Above, Kent Pegorsch; below, Tom Charlesworth.)

Sometime after 1901, Irving Lord built the Electric Dock (shown above) between the Grand View Hotel and Wisconsin Veterans Home for riders of the Waupaca Electric Railway who took tour boats to reach other locations on the lakes. By 1911, Lord had added a picnic area and refreshment stand called Electric Park directly to the south across the trolley tracks. Dan Downey, owner of Waupaca Monument Works, and his wife, Maude, purchased the Electric Dock around 1915 and turned it into the Downey's Dock and boat livery (shown below). Dan had canoes and rowboats for rent and gave tours on his *Dan D.* motor launch. He also rented out cottages and acquired Electric Park sometime after 1925. After Dan passed away in 1931, followed by Maude in 1936, new owners ran the dock until the late 1940s. (Both, WHS.)

South from "Indian Crossing"
Chain o' Lakes,
Waupaca, Wis.

Charles Merriam moved to the eastern point between McCrossen and Nessling Lakes in 1898 with his wife, Amelia, and stepdaughter, Bessie. By 1901, he had purchased the *Lady of the Lake* steamer (shown above) from William Smith and operated it with young Bessie—Charles put coal and wood in the engine while Bessie piloted. Passengers enjoyed Charles's friendly humor, giving him the nickname Captain Merriam, and his business prospered. Over the next decade, Charles purchased two gasoline-powered passenger launches, the *May Flower* (later renamed the *Favorite*) and *Princess*, for Bessie to pilot. The *Lady of the Lake* became unusable in 1914, so Charles burned and sank the boat on Nessling Lake. However, it later floated up and remained in shallow water by the Merriams' property for many years. (Both, WHS.)

After Charles Merriam passed away in 1915, his stepdaughter, Bessie, managed the Chain o' Lakes Steamer & Cottage Co. and continued piloting the two gasoline launches. She met Edward Nelsen, an electrical engineer from Green Bay, on a launch ride, and they married in 1919. The couple (pictured at right in 1930) rebranded the business as Nelsen Boat Line and Cottages and built their own dock and storage facilities (shown below) on Rainbow Lake. They purchased a third gasoline launch, the *Rainbow*, and started offering canoes, rowboats, and Crystal River skiffs for rent. By the mid-1930s, the Nelsens had added an ice-cream and soft-drink parlor, picnic grounds, a bathhouse, and a bathing beach to their business. They purchased the *Normandie* motor launch to replace the *Rainbow* in 1937. (Right, Jack Bonnell, Skip Bonnell, and Kristi Diaz; below, WHS.)

This photograph shows Edward Nelsen posing with three patrons of Nelsen Boat Line and Cottages on a small gasoline launch he piloted for them on Rainbow Lake. Most small gasoline boats on the Chain o' Lakes had similar motors that powered a propeller at the back of the boat through a long pipe. These boats moved at about 20 mph, making them considerably faster than steamboats. (WHS.)

After Edward Nelsen passed away in 1939, his wife, Bessie, operated Nelsen Boat Line and Cottages for another eight years before selling it to Adrian and Dorothy Houck in 1947. The Houcks began renting boats with outboard motors and introduced their clipper launches (one is shown below) around 1950. They rebranded the business as Clipper Boat Line by 1953 and ran it until the end of the decade. (WHS.)

John R. Edmunds operated his 25-foot-long steamer named the *Glide* (shown above) after moving to the Chain o' Lakes area in 1903 with his wife, Jennie, and two of his children, Benjamin and Hobert. To compete with the other steamboats on the lakes, John advertised the *Glide* as incredibly safe, even claiming that its engine would not blow up, and placed life-preserver cushions on the seats. He also installed a light on the front of the boat to give tours at night, making him the only steamer captain to do so. John Edmunds stopped running the boat when he was admitted to the Waupaca County Asylum in Royalton in the late 1910s; he died there in 1920 at age 62. (Above, Bob and Mary Ann Wells; below, WHS.)

Following in the footsteps of his father, John R. Edmunds, Hobert "Hobie" Edmunds gave tours of the lakes in a 25-foot gasoline launch at age 13 in 1909, then purchased his own gasoline launch, the *Anna* (pictured above), three years later. Hobert's tours were so popular that in 1915, he commissioned Joseph Terrio of Waupaca to build the *Mandalay*, a 36-foot-long motor launch that seated 40 people. The below photograph shows the *Mandalay* picking up Camp Onaway participants and counselors in 1923. Hobert served in the US Army from 1917 to 1919, during World War I, and survived the sinking of the SS *Tuscania* after a German submarine torpedoed it off the coast of Ireland in 1918. He was married to Mayme Stuehmer of Waupaca by 1920. (Above, WHS; below, BGB.)

Hobert Edmunds purchased land on Taylor Lake in the 1920s and opened his boat livery, Edmunds' Dock and Boat Line (pictured above), which included a covered dock with a refreshment stand, several boathouses, and picnic grounds. As his business boomed, Edmunds commissioned five additional gasoline launches—the *Mandalay II* and *Mandalay III*, *North Star*, *Starlight*, and *Viking* (pictured below)—and rented out canoes, rowboats, and Crystal River boats. Edmunds also bought one of the first Chris-Craft runabouts on the Chain o' Lakes and gave passengers speedy "thrill rides." He sold the boat livery in 1955. (Above, WHS; below, Tom Charlesworth.)

After his first wife, Mayme, died in 1934, Hobert Edmunds married Ethel Jorgensen (pictured) of Poy Sippi, Wisconsin, two years later. In 1937, they had their only child, Don, who contracted polio when he was eight years old. Even though the disease paralyzed his legs, Don relearned how to walk and became a state trapshooting champion in his 20s. (WHS.)

This photograph shows Hobert Edmunds's *North Star* delivering supplies to Camp Onaway. From the 1920s to the 1950s, Edmunds ferried campers, staff, and supplies to Onaway Island and took the boys on Crystal River trips, growing close with the staff and members of the Boys' Brigade of Neenah in the process. After selling Edmunds' Dock and Boat Line, Edmunds worked as the caretaker at Camp Onaway in 1956 and 1957. (BGB.)

Tourists and locals began taking trips down the Crystal River in small wooden skiffs in the 1890s. Fred and William Smith regularly organized trips for their hotel guests, and the activity became so popular that every Chain o' Lakes boat livery offered trips by the 1920s. Launches would drop participants and their canoes at the mouth of the Crystal River in Long Lake in the morning and pick them up at Parfreyville, Little Hope, or Waupaca in the late afternoon or evening. Boaters rode the river as it moved southeast to Rural and then northeast toward Waupaca, stopping to eat lunch, fish, or swim along the way. These photographs show a group of Camp Cleghorn vacationers on a Crystal River trip around 1920. (Both, the family of Herbert Wenberg.)

People who take the Crystal River trip today are well aware of how frustrating navigating the river's rapids can be, especially after tipping over repeatedly. Early boaters on the river probably had a rougher time, since locals had yet to tame the river by removing rocks or widening and deepening it. The 1923 photograph above shows two Camp Onaway boys trying to free their canoe from some brush along the Crystal River's shore before it sinks. The 1930s image at left shows two girls heading straight into a patch of rocks while riding some of the river's wild rapids. These canoes were much heavier than the plexiglass ones used today, so tipping them over to dump out any water would have required a lot of strength. (Above, BGB; left, WHS.)

This photograph from the early 1920s shows one of the gasoline launches that delivered Crystal River trip participants and their canoes to the mouth of the river in Long Lake. This complimentary ride through the scenic Chain o' Lakes relaxed boaters before they took on the raging river. (Kent Pegorsch.)

On July 30, 1916, people from all over the east-central Wisconsin area gathered at the Grand View Hotel to watch a regatta that included inboard motorboat, outboard motorboat, canoe, rowboat, and swimming races. This photograph shows two boats nearing the finish line in the five-mile motorboat race while the excited crowd eagerly watches from the hotel's dock. (WHS.)

Although swimming on the Chain o' Lakes did not change much from the 1880s onward, the clothing tourists wore to swim changed drastically. At the turn of the century, women wore ankle-length skirts and long-sleeved blouses, while men wore garments resembling union suits. One-piece tank suits for men and suits with shorter sleeves and skirts for women appeared on the market in the 1910s. Women donned more form-fitting suits in the 1930s that were much shorter and almost indistinguishable from men's suits. Before the introduction of Lycra and nylon swimsuits in the 1960s, companies mainly made swimsuits out of wool because of its water-repelling properties. Above, a family swims at Locksley Lodge in the early 1920s, and below, a group of Crystal River swimmers poses in the 1930s. (Above, Kent Pegorsch; below, WHS.)

Runabouts—small four-to-ten-passenger boats usually made of varnished wood—became popular among middle-class boaters in the 1920s and 1930s. These boats were aerodynamically designed to quickly skim over the water and thrill passengers. Chris-Craft Boats of Michigan made most of the runabouts used by Chain o' Lakes boaters. Speeding and motorboat accidents soon became common, prompting the Wisconsin Legislature to establish a 15 mph speed limit on the lakes in 1941. The above image shows Betty Nelsen (later Bonnell), Bessie and Edward's only child, posing in the four-passenger Chris-Craft boat she drove for Nelsen Boat Line and Cottages in the late 1930s and 1940s. The below photograph shows a man driving a two-passenger runabout on Rainbow Lake in the 1940s. (Above, Jack Bonnell, Skip Bonnell, and Kristi Diaz; below, WHS.)

Several individuals started waterskiing in the 1920s, but the sport did not become widely popular until the 1940s, when Dick Pope Sr. promoted it at his Cypress Gardens theme park in Florida. Many Chain o' Lakes residents, including the young men shown in this 1940s photograph, made their own water skis and tried the sport after seeing photographs of Pope's skiers. (WHS.)

Sometime around 1940, Don Warner, a young Chain o' Lakes tourist, built a two-by-four-inch wooden board called an "aqua plane" with plans he found in an article. Boaters towed the board, and riders would stand up and balance on it to ride the waves. This photograph shows Ida Perry of Newdale Cottage riding an aqua plane in the 1940s. (Newdale Cottage Archives.)

This photograph shows Francis "Skipper" Cary of Waupaca riding his Roaring 40 hydroplane at 41.25 mph on Rainbow Lake in the 1940s. Cary piloted the first Chris-Craft boat owned by Edmunds' Dock and Boat Line and gained a reputation as a dangerous boater who drove too fast, even in the lakes' shallow channels. In 1949, he was arrested twice for exceeding the lakes' speed limit of 15 mph. (WHS.)

To enforce boating safety laws and speed limits on the Chain o' Lakes, the Waupaca County Sheriff's Department formed a water patrol to monitor the lakes in 1949. Arthur Krueger (pictured), a retiree of the Aluminum Company of America from Symco, became the Chain o' Lakes' first patrolman and served until 1970. (The Town of Farmington.)

In 1945, Gordon "Ding" Doerfler purchased swampy land on the southeastern shore of Limekiln Lake and opened the Ding's Dock boat livery (shown above) a year later. Doerfler suffered from polio as a child and was paralyzed from the waist down, but that did not stop him from building one of the Chain o' Lakes' most popular businesses. Ding's Dock rented out canoes, rowboats, fishing boats, motorboats, and aluminum boats; gave motor launch and Chris-Craft boat rides; and offered canoe trips on the Crystal River and Little Chain. The dock itself had a bait shop, snack shop, and picnic grounds. Doerfler ran the boat livery with the help of his wife, Connie Nelson (shown below), a Farmington native who had three summers of experience working at Edmunds' Dock and Boat Line. (Both, WHS.)

In 1955, Ding Doerfler commissioned the Brooks Marine Company in Green Lake to build his first launch (shown above in 1975) and held a contest to decide the name of the boat. The winning entry was the *Connie Dee*, an homage to Ding's wife, Connie. A few years later, Doerfler bought two of the launches from the Clipper (formerly Nelsen) Boat Line after it closed and renamed them the *Connie Dee II* and *Connie Dee III*. He used the boats to give tours and tow skiffs to the Crystal River. In 1973, Ding sold the business to his employee of 11 years, Joe Leean, who moved the business to its present location on Columbia Lake in 1980. The 1968 photograph below shows Ding (seated, second from right) with Joe and his wife, Ginny (both standing). (Both, Joe and Ginny Leean.)

The photograph at left shows young Edward Browne holding an impressive Northern Pike he caught around 1910, while the below photograph shows Doris Charlesworth posing with a trout she caught in the 1950s. Locals began fishing on the Chain o' Lakes for fun—instead of necessity—in the 1870s, and although fishing equipment and boats became more advanced over time, the activity itself has changed little. Early promoters of the lakes tried to persuade potential fishermen to visit by stressing how easy it was to catch a variety of big pickerel, black bass, perch, and trout in a single afternoon. State and local conservation groups have worked hard since the 1870s to keep the lakes well stocked with fish for the enjoyment of visitors. (Left, WHS; below, Tom Charlesworth.)

Norman and Betty Prell of Stevens Point took over the Camp Cleghorn boat livery in 1949, renaming it Prell's Boat Livery (shown above). Betty, the daughter of Arthur and Ada Charlesworth, grew up staying at her family's cottage at Camp Cleghorn, and Norman's parents and sister took over the camp's store in 1946. Prell's rented out canoes, rowboats, and motorboats and sold gas to boaters. In 1955, the livery started selling and servicing boats (and, later, snowmobiles) made by Evinrude Motors, a Milwaukee company. In 1978, the Prells sold the business to Bruce Becker, who opened an additional location (shown below in 2019) at the former site of Ding's Dock on Limekiln Lake by 1986. Becker later closed the Camp Cleghorn location and renamed the business Becker's Marina. (Above, WHS; below, author's collection.)

In the late 1950s, Ding Doerfler of Ding's Dock commissioned the building of 24 pine riverboats coated with fiberglass resin to prevent leaking. LaVerne "Wormy" Nelson, owner of Edmunds' Dock and Boat Line from 1955 until the early 1960s, then made a mold of one of the boats and built one completely made of fiberglass. Nelson and Doerfler started using the fiberglass skiffs (shown above) in 1960 and 1961, respectively. Although boaters could easily paddle and lift these skiffs, they were hard to control. Therefore, careening into rocks and the resulting injuries became staples of the Crystal River trip. The 1982 photograph at left shows Joy Kraemer nursing a shin injury while posing with her sister, Jill (standing, second from left), and friends during one such trip. (Above, Waupaca Area Public Library; left, author's collection.)

A group of 16 locals formed the Chain o' Lakes Water Ski Club in 1961 to promote the sport in the area, providing waterskiing lessons and organizing shows for about three years. The club reemerged in 1972 when three local water skiers—Bob Lund, Pete Meiklejohn, and Pat Meighan —founded the Chain Skiers team (pictured above and below in 2019). The group began giving free shows during the summer on Rainbow Lake in front of the Wisconsin Veterans Home that featured barefoot skiing, trick skiing, jumps, double acts, pyramids, and other stunts. Member Wayne Colden closed out many shows by holding on to a kite attached to a boat that took off and pulled him into the air. Today, the Chain Skiers still perform and continue the tradition of teaching the sport to the community by hosting "learn to ski" days. (Both, the Chain Skiers.)

In 1962, Earl C. Brien, a summer resident of Taylor Lake, launched a seven-passenger replica of a sternwheeler paddleboat that he named the *Hester B* after his wife. He designed and built the boat on his own, using two pontoons to keep it afloat and a gasoline engine to power the paddle wheel. Joe Leean, a Wisconsin state senator from 1984 to 1995 and former owner of Ding's Dock, later purchased the vessel and renamed it the *Senate Chambers*. Leean organized races between the *Chief Waupaca* and *Senate Chambers* on Rainbow Lake to raise money for his campaigns. In the early 2000s, Leean rebuilt the boat, replaced the pontoons, and installed a diesel engine. The 2000s photograph above shows Leean on the *Senate Chambers* with his wife, Ginny, and friends; Joe and Ginny are the couple at right. The below photograph shows the same boat in 2019. (Above, Joe and Ginny Leean; below, author's collection.)

In 1973, Joe Leean of Ding's Dock and Pat Meighan, his employee, bought the *Chief Oshkosh* (shown above), a 65-foot-long replica of the *Paul L.* sternwheeler that traveled in Lakes Poygan and Butte des Morts from 1907 to 1923. The Chief Oshkosh Brewing Company commissioned the Schwarz Marine Company of Two Rivers to build the *Chief Oshkosh* in 1963 to transport beer along the same route as the *Paul L.* but gave it away after two years. Subsequent owners used the boat for different purposes until it broke down in 1970 and remained docked in Lake Butte des Morts. Leean and Meighan sawed the *Chief Oshkosh* out of the lake during the winter of 1973–1974, took it apart, and transported it to Ding's Dock on a flatbed truck, as shown in the below photograph. (Both, Joe and Ginny Leean.)

During the spring of 1974, Joe Leean and Pat Meighan completely refurbished the *Chief Oshkosh* at Ding's Dock, as shown above. They enclosed the lower cabin, replaced the railings on the upper deck, and installed a gas engine to power the wheel. The boat, newly christened the *Chief Waupaca* (shown below), began giving tours of the Chain o' Lakes that summer and docked at Ding's Dock. In 1975, Leean and Meighan purchased the Edmunds' Dock and Boat Line property, which they renamed Clear Water Harbor, on Taylor Lake and docked the boat there. The *Chief Waupaca* became so popular that they gave regular tours of the upper lakes four times a day, seven days a week during the summer season and rented out the boat for private events. Pat Meighan and his wife, Mimi, became the first couple to get married on the boat. (Both, Joe and Ginny Leean.)

After Pat Meighan purchased Joe Leean's share of Clear Water Harbor in 1979, he demolished most of the old Edmunds' Dock and Boat Line buildings and renovated the boat showroom into a bar and restaurant with a deck facing Taylor Lake. Pat and his wife, Mimi, turned the Harbor (pictured above in 2019) into the entertainment hot spot of the Chain o' Lakes, offering tasty food, classic drinks, live music, and a laid-back environment for people of all ages. In 1983, with tours on the *Chief Waupaca* in high demand, the Meighans commissioned the construction of a smaller passenger boat (shown below) that could pass under the Indian Crossing bridge and tour the lower lakes. They named the vessel *Lady of the Lakes* after William Smith and Charles Merriam's old steamboat *Lady of the Lake*. (Above, author's collection; below, Clear Water Harbor.)

The Lady of the Lakes

Visit us at
arcadiapublishing.com

CPSIA information can be obtained
at www.ICGtesting.com
Printed in the USA
LVHW071731090820
662759LV00017B/1665